Scarf Tying
Magic

"Bobbie Jean Thompson's book, *Scarf Tying Magic* is long overdue! Because of my heavy travel schedule, I especially love Bobbie Jean's 'Scarf Magic Travel Roll'—great for packing scarves. Her book is a wealth of information and a must for any woman who has thought scarves were more of a bother than a pleasure. I especially love the 'fan.' It brings compliments every time."

Carole Jackson

Author of *Color Me Beautiful, Color for Men* and *the Color Me Beautiful Makeup Book*

"Every outfit needs that special, finishing touch. Scarves can often provide that touch, but many women hesitate to purchase them because they don't know how to tie them in interesting ways.

In this informative book, Bobbie Jean Thompson has solved that problem by presenting many ways to tie scarves, with clear instructions and clever illustrations. She takes the guesswork out of accessorizing through the use of scarves tied in imaginative ways.

You will also find other great ideas for choosing and using scarves. So cast off your fear of scarf-tying, and "tie one on"!"

Gerrie Pinckney

Author of *New Image for Women*
President, Fashion Academy Inc.

"Like color, scarves are the signature stamp of your own personality. *Scarf Tying Magic* is a fast and easy approach to adding the finishing touch to any woman's style."

Clare Revelli

Designer and Author of the book
and video, *Color and You*

Bobbie Jean Thompson's

Scarf Tying *Magic*

ACROPOLIS BOOKS LTD.
WASHINGTON, D.C.

This book is dedicated with special appreciation: To my children, *Mark and Tamela Tiffin* for their love, patience, support, enthusiasm and humor who have added magic to my life. I am so thankful and privileged to be their Mom . . . which is my greatest accomplishment. *Mark* has always exhorted me to "Knock-em-Dead, Mom." *Tamela* has always been my beautiful model for the scarves and fashion.

To, my parents, *Virginia Jean and Oral Spry* who bought me my first magical scarf, which was the beginning of *"Scarf Tying Magic."* They have given me the God given gift of self-worth and have always been there to support, love and care for me in every way.

To, my husband, *Dr. Ron* (as he's known in the Image Industry) who has believed, helped, supported, managed, counseled, pasted, glued, readied, carried, pushed, promoted and held my hand. You name it . . . *Ron* has done it for my success. He has lead me and is the one person who has made it all happen. I can't quite put into words exactly how much he means to me and all my projects, but I think he knows. I've heard it said, "Gee, What A Great Team They Make!!" I have to agree, because without his patience, encouragement, wisdom, wit, interest, dedication, understanding and love I would not have a **Magical** life.

Are there Acropolis books you want but cannot find in your local stores?
You can get any Acropolis book title in print. Simply send title and retail price. Be sure to add postage and handling: $2.25 for orders up to $15.00; $3.00 for orders from $15.01 to $30.00; $3.75 for orders from $30.01 to $100.00; $4.50 for orders over $100.00. District of Columbia residents add applicable sales tax. Enclose check or money order only, no cash please, to:

ACROPOLIS BOOKS LTD.
2400 17th St., N.W.
WASHINGTON, D.C. 20009

Library of Congress Cataloging-in-Publication Data
Thompson, Bobbie Jean
  Scarf tying magic.

  Includes index.
  1. Scarves. I. Title.
TT667.5.T48 1988   646   88-12278
ISBN 0-87491-906-1
ISBN 0-87491-892-8 (pbk.)

Illustrations by
REMCO, Roy McClanahan and Bobbie Jean Thompson

Director of Photography
Tamela Tiffin Thompson

Cover and book designed by
Pamela Moore

ACROPOLIS BOOKS LTD.
Alphons J. Hackl, Publisher
Colortone Building, 2400 17th St., N.W.
Washington, D.C. 20009

Printed in the United States of America by
COLORTONE PRESS
Creative Graphics, Inc.
Washington, D.C. 20009

Attention: Schools and Corporations ACROPOLIS books are available at quantity discounts with bulk purchase for educational, business, or sales promotional use. For information, please write to: SPECIAL SALES DEPARTMENT, ACROPOLIS BOOKS LTD., 2400 17th St., N.W., Washington, D.C. 20009.

Table of Contents

Acknowledgments

In making this book possible I need to thank many because it has taken over two years to get to this stage. It's my belief that a book is never the work of one person, but many. . . . I wish to give my deepest appreciation to:

ACROPOLIS BOOKS, LTD.

Alphons Hackl, Publisher, for seeing the MAGIC of this book and wanting to publish it.

Sandy Trupp, Vice President/Publicity and my Managing Editor, for her helping, pushing, holding, leading me step by step of this publication. Sandy made me feel I really had a magical book.

John Hackl, Associate Publisher, for the creative thoughts on sales and productions.

The entire Staff for their GREAT work: *Pamela Moore,* Art Director, for the beautiful cover & proofing all the art work; *Jean Bernard ,* Editor, for going over the manuscript page by page; *Dan Wallace,* Director of Marketing, for his creative advice.

Roy McClanahan, Graphic Designer, for endless time and work. Best of all, for having a good attitude in agreeing to change and redo things the way I wanted.

Sid Scallet, my personal editor, for his knowledge, talent and professional efficiency.

Mona Simpson, my personal associate, for her assistance and always being there when I need her.

Image Reflections Consultants for their encouragement, with enthusiasm, time spent in our seminars and just being part of the Image Reflections team. Especially the gals from the Colors & You Boutique, *Shirley Hammond* and *Carolyn Allie*, Roanoke, VA.

Personal Clients, Friends and Relatives for helping to get me into flight on this "Magic Carpet" with their friendship and vote of confidence. A special thanks to cousin, *Lillian Marsden,* for her loyalty and always going the extra mile for me.

Alphagraphics Printshop for printing the hundreds of copies of the original *"Scarf Tying Magic"* before this printing. Thanks *Stuart* and *Marilu Thomas* and *Kurt Ayan.*

The Image Company for the photographs.

Time Out Productions for the New Special Effects Scarf Tying Magic Video. Special thanks to *Bryan Williams* for the studio and location shooting, the endless hours of editing and putting the special effects together for the New Scarf Tying Magic Video.

Lee Mulvaney, Kelly Reeves, Dawn Lawrence and especially *Josephine Gibson* of Pixels who diligently typed, retyped and formatted the original manuscript.

Scarf and Accessories Companies for creating beautiful accessories . . . Karla Jordon Kollections, Accessory Street, Echo, Gennie Johansen, Marlo Silks, Colors with Flair, Dina Kohn, Vera and countless Designers.

The Models for their own magic with scarves: *Mona Simpson, June Knight, Sandra Williams, Dawn Lawrence, Betty Fox, Betty Ferguson, Linda Jones, Eleanor Droney, Patsy Wood, Daisy and Jennifer Wright* and the most important a professional model, my daughter, *Tamela Tiffin Thompson,* the producer and director of the photo shoot.

The *Leaders in the Image Field* who have commented about this book. They are remarkable women with many accomplishments in the Image, Color and Accessory industry.

Last put by no means least, *GOD,* for the wonderful opportunity to live a life and have a career with many blessings of helping others feel better about themselves. GOD is the one who is the inspiration of all Ideas. The one who gives life the mystery of magic.

Introduction

Scarves are SUPER . . . SURPRISING . . . SPLENDID . . . SCRUMPTIOUS . . . Yes, using a scarf correctly means sensational styling savvy!

Scarves are the most unusual accessory you can use to be creative with your clothing. After you've taken the time to learn a few basic tying methods, you can produce a look that is yours alone.

You can invest a small amount of time and money to gain great joy in the art of dressing with scarves. When you learned to tie an overhand knot as a child, you were taking the first step toward learning how to tie a scarf. Now is the time to build on what you have learned. It does take some practice, but the benefits of learning about the world of scarves and scarf tying are so rewarding and wonderful that the practice will be well worth it.

In my own life, scarves have played a special role in reflecting my image. I never realized why I enjoyed wearing scarves when I was growing up. Now I understand why. It's not only because I love the magic of the scarf; it's also because I have a lot of space between my chin and shoulders. In other words, I have a long neck to tie one on.

I have always had a long neck—even as a young child. Of course, then I didn't realize I had a long neck. I can remember how I adored my junior high school's cheerleading uniform that had a skirt and a V-neck sweater. I do recall feeling better as a cheerleader, however, whenever I wore our school scarf around my neck. I felt more secure with the scarf tucked in and around my cheerleader's V-neck sweater. This was the beginning of scarf magic for me.

My honeymoon trosseau included a wardrobe of scarves. I wore them as shawls for the evening, around my neck, and as head wraps after swimming. Scarves can do wonders for your looks when you have wet hair.

When I modeled professionally, I always had scarves in my model's hat bag. The scarves were used in many ways. I would drape one around my shoulders when it was chilly, and tie my hair back in a turban when I did a beach shot in Miami. I always tied it around my head—literally over my entire head, covering my hair, head, and face; bringing the ends around the back of my head and neck; and tying the ends around my chin. I used this over-the-head cap wrap when removing garments for fashion shows. Not only did this ensure that I would not get makeup on the clothing I was modeling, it also protected my makeup and hairstyling.

After my daughter Tamela was born, I practiced motherly duties by sewing mother-daughter dresses. I'd also make matching scarves for our outfits. One day I had about 29 inches left from the end of some material of a dress I had made. I wanted to make a bias scarf to tie around my head, but I didn't have enough material. What could I do? Well, I devised a way of making a bias scarf out of a piece of material that was about 29 by 11 inches. The fabric was not large enough to make a square scarf or a triangular one, and it was not long enough to make the rectangular shape I wanted. I made that bias scarf (and I still have it today!). The trick I used in making this unusual scarf is unique—and I think you'll like it. I've made many "short material" bias scarves since then. Full details and drawings are in the appendix.

My point is this: My love for scarves inspired me on that day— has always inspired me—to see in even the "meanest" piece of leftover material the possibility of scarf-making. When you discover what scarves can mean for you, you too will become inspired by their possibilities.

I have learned even more about scarves over the years by teaching my Scarf Tying Magic classes. I travel the world as president of the Image Reflections Company, giving classes, seminars, and lectures. In my classes I always stress the value of scarves. It was nice being called the "Scarf Lady" on my recent seminar lecture tour of Australia.

It never occurred to me that I should write a book about scarves until I discovered that not everyone knew about them—their magic—and how to use scarves. I came to the conclusion that, even if others did know about scarves, I had to do this book. It's not what you know, after all, but what you DO with what you know that matters. I feel that I can help everyone understand better how to use scarves to complete and complement their look.

A scarf is an accent that can add exciting versatility to your wardrobe. It's not just an accessory. It's a **NE-CES-SORY!!** Yes, I said **necessory,** not just accessory. You see, a scarf is truly a necessity, because it can change a basic outfit in so many different ways, creating a world of different looks. You can do all sorts of extraordinary things with an ordinary scarf.

You can belt, clip, drape, fold, knot, loop, pin, pull, push, sash, stuff, tie, tuck, twist, or wrap a scarf to change, update, and add sparkle to your look.

There's no failure in scarf-tying except in not trying. This book contains some old favorite ties—and some new tricks with scarves that you can learn. It can teach you some tricks for those KNOTS THAT ARE NOT FOR NAUGHT. You will learn to express your style through scarves and add a hallmark to your signature.

So let's get started learning about and practicing the illusions that you can create through SCARF-TYING MAGIC!!

1. Selecting Your Scarves

What should you consider when selecting a scarf? Actually, what you should consider is not unlike what you usually consider when you choose a garment for your body. But before we get down to the specifics of scarf-selection, let's give some thought to what a scarf can do for you—and what it has always done.

A scarf is the most wonderful accessory you can own. Everyone can learn to wear scarves. No matter what your body size or shape is, there is a scarf size and shape for you. You should become a collector of different kinds of scarves. As a matter of fact, you need to have a wardrobe of scarves.

The scarf was handed down from Biblical days. The ancient Greeks, Romans, Indians, knights, and Normans knew how a scarf could be used: as a stole or shawl, a shoulder wrap, over the head as a turban, draped around the neck, wrapped around the waist, stuffed in a pocket, looped to form a hat. As the Egyptians, Assyrians, Persians, and those before us have learned, there are as many ways to use a scarf as the imagination allows.

Wearing scarves sometimes takes a little courage. But once you take the first step with a scarf and the compliments come your way, and you begin to discern how positive you feel wearing one, you will have no trouble making scarves an integral part of your wardrobe. And, of course, the beauty of the scarf is that you can wear it over and over again using it in different ways to create an endlessly number of effects.

Let's now consider some of the specific things you should consider when trying to select a scarf.

There are seven categories for scarf-selection:

Shape: What shape do you want or need? Will the shape complement the outfit you are wearing?

Size: What size scarf should you select for your body proportion? Should it be long or short, wide or narrow?

Color: What color should you select for your skin, hair, and eyes? What color do you need to coordinate the scarf with the rest of your wardrobe?

Quality: What quality of scarf do you need for your wardrobe? What degree of quality do you want to project with the scarf?

Fabric: What type of fabric do you want for your scarf? Do you want a soft silk? Or, would the heavier texture of a nubby wool scarf be best?

Expression of Style: What type of scarf do you need to express the style that you want to achieve? Do you want a romantic, casual, or dramatic look?

Lifestyle: What sort of activities would you be doing when you wear a scarf? What kind of work do you do? What do you do for recreation?

Let's discuss each of the seven categories in greater detail.

Shape

The three basic shapes for scarves are rectangle, square, and bias.

Rectangle

The rectangular shaped scarf is one that has four sides and four right angles. Its length is greater than its width. The rectangle scarf is also called an oblong.

Many people deem the rectangle scarf the most versatile. It is one that can be used and tied in more ways than any other scarf. It's considered to be more ornamental than functional.

The Rectangle (Oblong) Shape
Length greater than width having
four sides with four right angles.
The sizes vary and are not meant
for warmth (except the wool ones)
but for accentuation.

This scarf can be used to create wonderful lateral optical illusions. When tied in a vertical fashion, it elongates the body, making one appear taller and thinner.

One's body proportion should dictate how long or short the rectangle scarf should be. A tall person can wear a much longer scarf than a petite person.

Square

The square shaped scarf is one with four equal sides and four right angles. Its length and its width are the same.

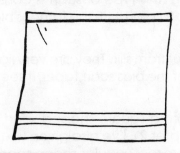

The Square Shape
Length and width are the same
with four equal sides and four right
angles.
The square shape scarf is in many
sizes. It can be folded into a
rectangular shape.

I have heard it said that a square scarf is not very versatile, but in fact a larger square scarf can be used quite nicely for ornamentation or warmth—and it's immensely functional. Depending on its size, a square scarf can be much more functional than other shapes. It can be tied, draped, and even used as a garment in itself. It can easily serve as a halter, blouse, or sarong, or even as a dress cover-up for the beach. It's great for filling in a suit or neck-line. The square can even be folded into a rectangle or bias-shaped scarf.

The optical illusion that a square-shaped scarf can create at the neck is a wonderful horizontal. This helps to balance a long neck, narrow shoulders, and/or a small bust.

Bias

The bias-shaped scarf looks like a rectangle shape with diagonal ends. It is achieved by cutting the fabric diagonally across its grain.

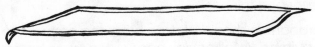

The Bias Shape
A slanting or diagonal cut of fabric which is across the weave of cloth. This gives a flowing, fluid, graceful curve movement with slenderizing effects.

Often called the "fashion scarf," this type of scarf is considered modern in its look. It came into fashion with the famous bias-cut garments of the 1920s.

Most bias scarves seem to be cut from silk. They are very light, soft, airy, and fluid. Since the ends of the bias scarf taper, it seems to glide with the body.

You can make a bias scarf from a square-shaped scarf by folding it in a certain way (see chapter 2). I've also given you instructions for making a bias scarf from rectangular-shape scarf or fabric (see the Appendix).

The optical illusion created by a bias scarf is very slimming. Of course, this slenderizing effect can provide a big bonus to your wardrobe. You can learn to take pounds off by putting a bias scarf on!

Size

You must think of the size of the scarf in relation to your body proportion. Your body measurements are the primary guide in determining the scarf size that will work best for you.

However, you must consider how you plan to wear the scarf. Will it be the size you need, for instance, to go around your hips if you want to create a Butterfly Sarong? Is it too large to go around your neck? Is it small enough to serve as a pocket ornament?

Sizes of scarves vary depending on their shape. Consider the following guidelines for size for selecting your scarves.

Rectangle

The rectangle scarf size of a **long** scarf varies from 64 × 10 inches to 72 × 11 inches. The size looks best on a tall or large person. The long rectangle is great for the Eye of the Needle.

The **middle** size of a rectangle scarf ranges from about 25 × 8 inches to about 54 × 11 inches. This is the best **all-around** size for a rectangle scarf. The middle-size scarf is wonderful for so many ties, from the Square Knot to the Band-O-Tie.

The **small** size of a rectangle scarf is around 46 × 5 inches to 44 × 3 inches. This size is tied nicely under the neck collar into a Windsor Knot or the Duchess of Windsor.

The rectangle scarf works as a bow, a filler for jackets and coats, a belt, a muffler, an ascot, a head wrap, and many other fashion ties.

Square

The **large** square scarf usually measures 45 × 45 inches or 56 × 56 inches up to 60 × 60 inches. This size works beautifully for the Secret Shawl Knot, the Armadillo Wrap, and the Throw Wraps or Butterfly Sarong.

The **middle**-sized square scarf ranges from 27 × 27 inches to 36 × 36 inches. It can be used for added warmth as a Square Knot. The Bandit is also good for this size. And perfect for this size is the Hal-Blouse-Ter.

The square size that measures 24 × 24 inches or smaller has limited uses. It can be employed as a filler for V-necks, and it's marvelous for the collar-choker. A square pocket scarf is one that measures anywhere from 18 × 18 inches down to 6 × 6 inches. The Square Pocket scarf that has laces around it can be used to add a more romantic look to a business suit when placed in the outside breast pocket with the point of the scarf going up. It can also be used on the lapel of a jacket. Fold it into a small triangle and pin it, with a small fashion pin, so that the larger points are going down.

Bias

This is the size of scarf that is longer that it is wide. The optical illusion that is created from the bias-cut makes the scarf appear even longer.

The **long** bias scarf is around 70 × 9 inches. The **middle** size is about 59 × 7 inches, which is the basic size for the bias scarf. A **small** bias scarf measures about 42 × 7 inches.

Color

The color of your scarf is a very important consideration. A scarf's color needs to harmonize in two areas. First, it must blend with your **personal color pattern.** Second, it needs to match the garment you're wearing.

Every woman possesses a color pattern, which consists of her hair, eye, and skin colors. You can have a predominant color pattern that is **cool** (blue) or **warm** (golden yellow). The personal color pattern is also known as the **seasonal concept** of color pattern. Looked at from this concept, your color pattern fits into one of the four seasons. Within your season there is the light, bright, dark, muted, and clear.

The scope of color is broken down into three different areas: hue, intensity, and value.

Hue is just the name of the color itself.

Intensity is the clarity of the color. It refers to how brightly or how dully the color is revealed.

Value is the lightness or darkness of the color.

The color of your scarves should not only blend with your seasonal color patterns (your hair, skin, and eye color), it also should harmonize with your garment. After learning your color season, you should consider what color/colors in a scarf would work best with the outfit you have on.

When you wear solid colors it is easier to select a scarf color, since many scarves are made with more than one color. If you are wearing a solid color garment, it is fun to add spice to your look by selecting a printed paisley, or geometrically patterned scarf. If your wardrobe is mainly in patterns, prints, or plaids, you will want to select scarves that are mainly solid colors.

When you feel confident and comfortable wearing your scarves, then try mixing patterns on patterns. Study how designers use patterns and you'll be able to achieve this skill for yourself. I have become brave and now I love to mix patterns. It does take a little more creativity to mix and make it work. The key to putting a mixed look together is always to come up with a combination of colors that is the same for the outfit and the scarf.

Quality

In selecting a scarf there are certain distinctive features to consider in quality. The three main areas you want to think about are **design, workmanship, and fabric.**

The label on the scarf will give you the designer's name, which will in turn give you an indication of the quality of the scarf. However, I have occasionally found designer scarves to be overpriced for their quality. So don't always let a well-known name be your guide in choosing a scarf.

In looking at the **design** of a scarf you can observe how everything in the scarf works—or doesn't work—together. If the scarf has a stamped or pressed design, is the design covering the entire scarf? If the scarf has been hand-printed, do its colors all flow together the way you feel they should?

Does the design cover the scarf as a whole? I once saw a very expensive, large designer scarf on which a small part of the design was missing from the pattern on the scarf. Beware of this.

The **workmanship** of a scarf is its construction. The two main things you'll want to look at are the **cut** and the **hem.** Observe whether the scarf is cut correctly on the grain. Sometimes the cut is not straight.

The hem is the most important ingredient of workmanship. The highest quality hem is hand-rolled. It should be neat, even stitches—and they should be flat.

The seams around the scarf need to be straight; they should lie flat with no unraveling edge or puckering showing, should have no hanging threads. The thread should be of strong, high-quality natural fiber. Plastic thread is a substitute that pulls out easily and cheapens the scarf. It simply cries out that the workmanship has been poor.

The fabric of a scarf must be one of your more important considerations when choosing this accessory. A natural fiber is the highest quality material to have in a scarf. When you have a scarf with a label that says that the material is 100 percent natural wool, silk, or cotton, you have a scarf with the true mark of quality.

A scarf that is of good quality can last you a lifetime. You should buy the highest quality scarf that you can afford. Not only will it last longer, it also will look better.

Fabric

Recognizing the different fabrics of which scarves are made is quite necessary. The more you know about fabrics, the easier it is for you to make your scarf selections.

The fabric of a scarf is crucial in determining how you will wear it, whether you will be able to drape it and how, and whether the scarf will keep its shape and stay whole. In other words, will the fabric of the scarf serve as a long-term investment.

We generally classify scarf fabrics according to two major types of fibers: man-made or synthetic and the natural.

The **man-made** or synthetic fibers are nylon, rayon, polyester, and acrylic. These materials are often less luxurious and not as expensive as natural fibers. They are wonderful, care-free fabrics, however, that can save you much time and money. Some synthetic blends that are woven with natural fibers can combine the benefits of both types of fabrics. You can have a scarf that is also quite durable and easy to care for.

The **natural** fibers are cotton, wool, silk, and linen. The natural fabric scarf is the one I recommend. It will outlast a synthetic, and the elegance of natural material will always communicate good taste and high quality. Natural fabrics can also be luxurious as blends; however, when you have a blend, it should be 65 percent or more natural fiber.

The **cotton** scarf is usually made of oxford cloth, jersey, or piqué. It is smooth, sturdy, and absorbent. You usually will find cotton scarves in squares. I use most of my cotton scarves for tennis and casual wear. This fiber wrinkles easily, but it's wonderfully soft and comfortable to wear.

A **wool** scarf is very durable and holds its shape nicely. It gives you great warmth, it doesn't wrinkle as much, it resists dirt, and it's rain-resistant. It doesn't tear as easily as some of the other fabrics. It can be smooth, soft, firm, nubby, heavy, or light. In short, the wool scarf can be marvelously versatile—it's a great long-term investment. The wool scarf is usually expensive—but you should save your money so that you can have at least one in your wardrobe.

Silk is probably the most desirable scarf fabric. It is expensive, but its many superb qualities make it an excellent investment. It is smooth and soft—and the lightest of all the materials. It drapes over your body with grace and elegance. It is simply superb as an insulating fabric, and keeps you warm. It holds its shape quite well and is very strong.

There are many kinds of silk scarves: broadcloth, crêpe de Chine, organza chiffon, and others. The designs on silk scarves are stamped, silk-screened, hand-printed, and hand-painted. Because of its high quality, silk holds dyes quite well.

Many silks tend to wrinkle, so they need extra care. Most manufacturers recommend dry cleaning. However, I have had success hand-washing my silk scarves in Ivory Snow (see Chapter 4 for more details on washing silks and other scarf fabrics). Never wring or squeeze silk when you wash it.

The **linen** (or flax) scarf also conveys luxury and elegance. It is crisp-looking and very strong. Because it absorbs moisture quite well, it wears comfortably. It is not very wrinkle-resistant, however—a real disadvantage. Most linen scarves are made in smaller squares to serve as pocket ornaments or blouse bow ties.

Manufacturers usually recommend that linen be dry-cleaned, but it is really best to hand-wash the fabric in Ivory Snow. Do not wring it as you wash it; the washing wrinkles you put in the linen are very hard to remove. Iron it wet.

The fabric texture of a scarf can go from an open weave wool to a rayon blend to a smoothly flowing silk. Texture can add dimension to a scarf, particularly if it's nubby. When you dress with some texture in your scarf you create an interesting contrast. It's fun and exciting to coordinate and juxtapose different textures in one look. It takes a touch of courage and some creativity to mix textures in an outfit, but it can be so rewarding as you create an effect that is both coordinated and dynamic.

Expression of Style

One of the easiest ways to express your personal style is through the use of accessories, mainly scarves. It's not just the scarf itself that reflects your style, but the way you tie and wear it as well.

Your style is expressed as a result of your understanding two important things about yourself: your **physical characteristics** and your **basic personality.** The comfort of your style is really expressed from within.

In looking at your physical features, observe your bone structure: the shape of your face, eyes, nose, mouth; your hairstyle; and your age. Then consider your personality. Do you regard yourself as extroverted or introverted? The real trick is understanding who you are!

Much as been written about style and its various categories. Image artists have spoken about the **romantic,** the **casual,** the **natural,** the **dramatic,** the **professional,** the **glamorous,** the **artsy,** the **boyish,** the **faddish,** the **classic,** the **gamin,** the **delicate,** the **sexy,** the **statement maker,** and many others.

All of these descriptive categories are great, but the dominant factor you should ALWAYS consider when selecting a scarf to express your style is the situation and/or the occasion. In other words, it's important for you to understand your basic personality, but you must ultimately consider the occasion in which you will be revealing that basic personality. It's important to know **who** you are, but it's even more important to know **where** you are (or will be) when choosing the right scarf for the situation.

Lifestyle

Your lifestyle is different from your personal style. While your personal style reflects who you are, your lifestyle reflects what you do. You should try to achieve a balance between the two. If you can do so, then you will have an even better idea of the kinds of scarves that will work best for who you are and what you do.

To understand your lifestyle, you must determine what you spend your time doing and where you spend it. Do you work a nine-to-five job? If so, you'll need enough scarves to help you create lots of different looks. Do you do volunteer work? Is it outdoors? If so, you'll want to have textured, warm scarves for the cold climate. Do you find yourself in many dressy situations? If so, you will want to own formal chiffon scarves to wear over your head or shoulders as a shawl, or with your favorite fur coat.

One's lifestyle is forever changing. Your scarf wardrobe must change with it. You might change homes or your job, you will mature, you might find yourself growing interested in new volunteer work or having lots of new formal commitments as a result of your work or that of your spouse. As you and your environment change, you will want to select scarves that will work for the new you. Never give up a scarf, though, if it is correct for you. You never know when that old scarf you haven't worn for years may jump right out at you from deep in the closet and say, "Here I am! Wear me . . . I'm the best scarf you have for this occasion."

And of course, no matter how you change, you will want to be thought of as a unique person with her own unique style. And perhaps the best way to achieve that uniqueness is through the way you dress. Being well-dressed means taking the time for accessories and **necessories**—namely, THE SCARF.

Now that we have considered the seven elements involved in the correct selection of scarves that work best for you, it's high time we get cracking on the fun part of this book. Take the scarves that you have chosen and make them work **magic** for you as you develop your wardrobe and your look. Get your scarves out, put a tabletop mirror on the table and sit down in front of it. Start going through this book. Get down to practicing—doing these scarf ties. There's no time like the present. DO IT NOW! Use your scarves to create some **magic** with your **Scarf-Tying Magic!**

Sincerely Scarfing!!

Bobbie Jean

2. Tying Your Scarves

Now that you have selected your scarves and decided on certain color combinations for your wardrobe, it's time to learn how to tie one on. The excitement of understanding how versatile your scarves will be is wonderful! Taking one scarf and learning how to tie it in many different knots can transform your everyday outfits into something different day after day. Your image will be very distinctive.

The illustrated scarf ties that follow will help to get you started on an avenue of accessorizing. Take this *Scarf-Tying Magic* book, get in front of a mirror, or, even better, if you have a table top mirror, go to your kitchen table and start practicing. Why not make an appointment with yourself and spend an afternoon getting all tied up. . . .?

Take these ideas and build upon them to develop new ideas. Adapt one tie to another and create an entirely new and different look for yourself. There is no substitute for practicing how to tie scarves. Tie them, be comfortable with them, and then you will have the confidence to wear them. I hope that you will be able to use these ideas so that scarves will become part of you. Then you will not be "Fit To Be Tied . . . You'll Be Tied To Be Fit".

Three Basic Folds

from a square-shaped scarf

To make a triangular-shaped scarf

Start with a square-shaped scarf.
Take one pointed at a right angle
and fold it to the opposite right
angle.

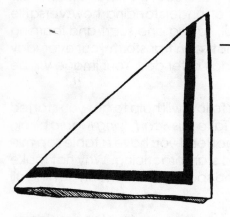

Fold to make a triangular shape.

To make a bias-shaped scarf

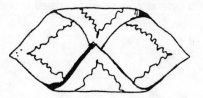

Take a square-shaped scarf and lay it down on a flat surface. Pick up two of the right angle corner points (one at a time) and bring to the center of the square.

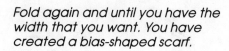

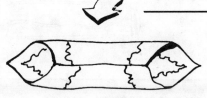

Fold the flat edge side down again to the center.

Fold again and until you have the width that you want. You have created a bias-shaped scarf.

To make a rectangular-shaped scarf

Fold one edge over to meet the other edge.

Continue to fold over. . .

. . .until you obtain the width you would like.

Lay a rectangular-shaped scarf, which is also called an oblong, on a flat surface. Fold the scarf over lengthwise.

Folding

Folding

Folding to the width that you want. You can make a narrow rectangle.

Tying Your Scarves

Square Knot

The square knot is a very important tie because so many ties come from it. The variations of this tie are almost endless. This tie can be tied two ways—depending if you are right- or left-handed. The rectangle illustrations will show how the scarf can be tied for a dominant left hand. The illustrations of the square knot will show the tie for a dominant right hand on pages 73 and 74 with a square-shaped scarf.

Begin with rectangle around the neck. . . This is for the dominant left hand. It can be tied the same way starting with the right side.

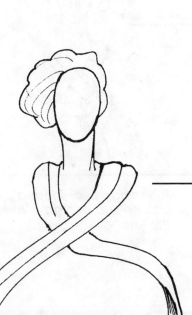

Bring the LEFT end OVER. . . the RIGHT panel. . . Up. . . Under. . . Through and TIE.

Take the end that's in the right
hand, which is the original left end,
and bring the RIGHT hand over the
LEFT.

This is a simple overhand knot,
What started as the left end is
now in your right hand.

. . . bring end UP. . .UNDER. . .
THROUGH and TIE.

This rectangular-shaped scarf
can be tied as high or as low to
the neck as you desire.

Remember: Left end over. Right up under and tie. Then, Right end over.
Left up under and tie.

Tying Your Scarves

Ascot

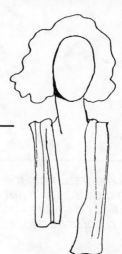

Put a rectangular-shaped scarf around your neck. One side is longer than the other.

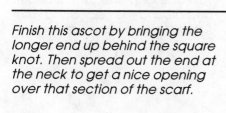

Tie a square knot.

Finish this ascot by bringing the longer end up behind the square knot. Then spread out the end at the neck to get a nice opening over that section of the scarf.

Muffler Collar

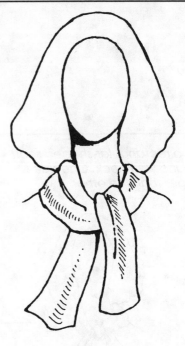

Complete the steps from the preceding drawing (with just an overhand tie or a square knot tie), and make a collar necklace.

Take the long end, twist it under and around the neck band. This forms a nice collar muffler.

Self-Covered Buttons from a Scarf

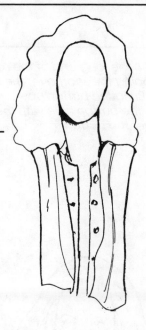

Put a rectangular-shaped scarf on the neck, keeping one end much longer.

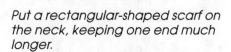

Secure the scarf with a square knot tie.

Bring the long end of the scarf up and under and over the knot and then spread it out.

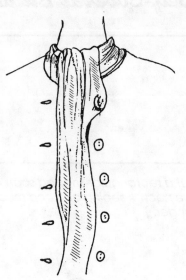

Work with the long end of the scarf by wrapping the scarf over the first button. Bring the button up through the button hole with the scarf over the button.

Repeat the same technique to cover as many or all the buttons you wish covered.

Eye of the Needle _____

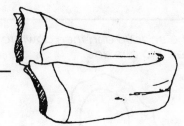

_____

Take a rectangular-shaped scarf
and fold it in half lengthwise.

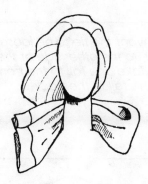

_____

Put the folded rectangular-
shaped scarf around the back of
your neck.

_____

Place the loop to one side and
open it up to bring the two ends
up through it.

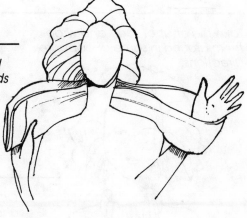

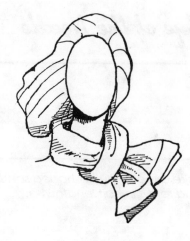

Pull the ends up and then down to tighten it to one side.

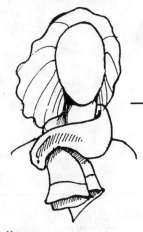

If you want the tie to be loose, just bring it to the other side of the neck. Take one tail to the front and one tail to the back.

Variations

Take the ends of scarf and wrap them around in same or opposite directions.

Or, continue wrapping to make a choker necklace.

Tying Your Scarves

Secret Eye of the Needle

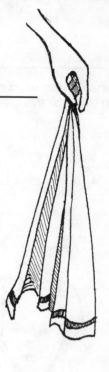

Pick up a rectangular-shaped scarf in the middle and hold with fingertips. You are holding it in the middle lengthwise.

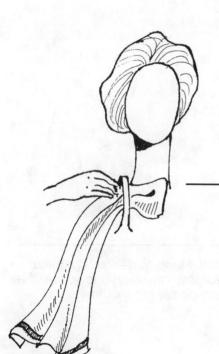

Pull the rectangular-shaped scarf under and through bra strap. If you are holding the scarf in your right hand, bring it under the right bra strap. The loop of the scarf is pointing in to your neck.

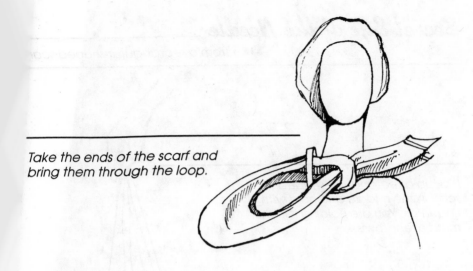

Take the ends of the scarf and bring them through the loop.

Pull the loop to desired tightness. Straighten the loop and secure the scarf across the shoulder.

Tying Your Scarves

Bunny Tail and Bunny Puff

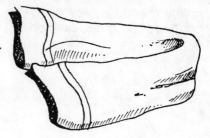

Take a rectangular-shaped scarf and fold it in half.;

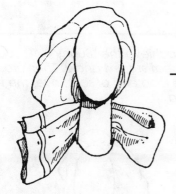

Place it around your neck.

Cross the tail end of the scarf over the loop end.

Bring the tail end up and then over the loop end. This is an overhand half knot.

Complete the "Bunny Tail" by
letting the tail ends flop over on
the top.

To achieve the "Bunny Puff" you
repeat steps 1 and 2. Then cross
the loop end of scarf over the tail
end.

Bring the loop end up and then
over the tail end. This is an
overhand half knot.

Complete the "Bunny Puff" by
letting the fluff loop flop over the
top.

Dog Cross

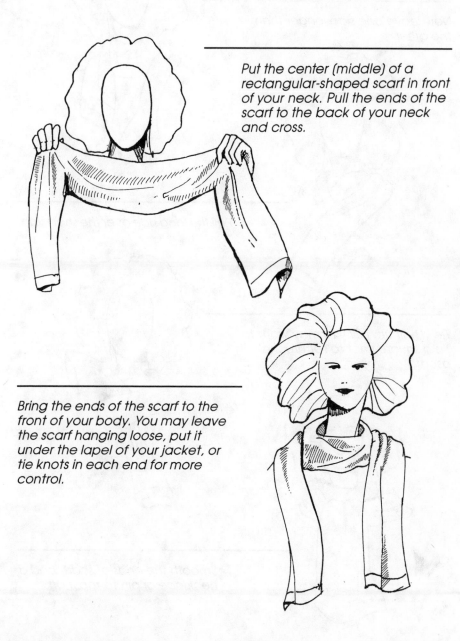

from a rectangular-shaped scarf

Put the center (middle) of a rectangular-shaped scarf in front of your neck. Pull the ends of the scarf to the back of your neck and cross.

Bring the ends of the scarf to the front of your body. You may leave the scarf hanging loose, put it under the lapel of your jacket, or tie knots in each end for more control.

Now leave one side longer than the other.

Pull the long side over the short side.

Tie a half tie. (Or you may want to tie a square knot to secure the ascot.)

Smooth the ends of scarf, add a necklace or pin to top it off.

Tying Your Scarves

Fluff-Puff

from a rectangular-shaped scarf

Place a rectangular-shaped scarf with the middle in front of the neck. Take the ends to the back of neck and cross. Bring the ends to the front. Pull the center of the scarf down to form a "Fluff-Puff"

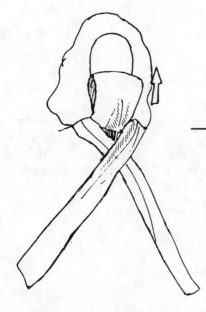

Take the panels (ends of scarf) and place them under the "Fluff-Puff" by crossing them.

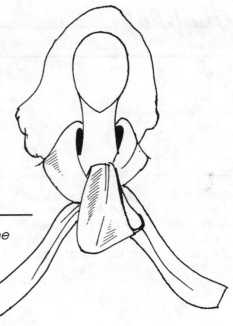

Bring the Fluff-Puff up and over the criss-crossed panels.

Then take the two end panels and bring them up and over. Complete the tie by tying a square knot on top of the "Fluff-Puff."

Tying Your Scarves

Duchess of Windsor

With a rectangular-shaped scarf, come about a third of the way up one end of the scarf. Tie a loose overhand knot.

Put the scarf around your neck, with the knot on one side.

Take the short side end and slide it down through the overhand knot. Tighten the overhand knot.

This looks like a man's tie. You can slide the knot up or down to wherever you want it.

Man's Full Windsor Knot

Put a rectangular-shaped scarf around your neck with one end longer. (The short tail should be on the right side of neck.)

You are working all the time with the long end. The left end is brought over the right part. Then up under and around. At this point you have a half knot tie.

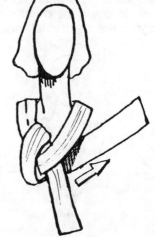

Hold the short end with your left hand; take the long end in your right hand. Bring the long end behind the short end.

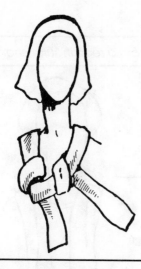

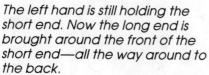

The left hand is still holding the short end. Now the long end is brought around the front of the short end—all the way around to the back.

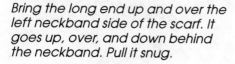

Bring the long end up and over the left neckband side of the scarf. It goes up, over, and down behind the neckband. Pull it snug.

Pull the long end down and straighter and tighten the knot then adjust the tails.

Fan

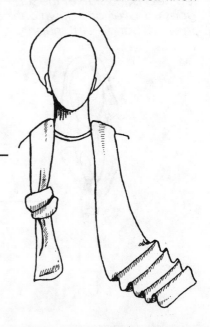

Place the rectangular-shaped scarf around your neck. Keep one end longer than the other.

Come one-third of the way up on the short end of the scarf and make a loose overhand self-knot.

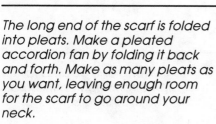

The long end of the scarf is folded into pleats. Make a pleated accordion fan by folding it back and forth. Make as many pleats as you want, leaving enough room for the scarf to go around your neck.

Tying Your Scarves

After pleating the long end to the desired length, drop one side of the pleated edge. Hold one end of the pleated side all together. This end is fed through the loose overhand knot, only halfway through.

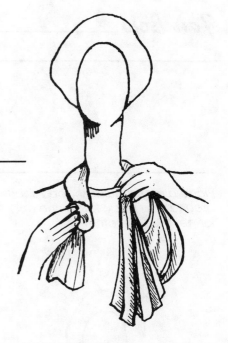

After feeding the pleated end halfway through the overhand knot, pull the short end down, and tighten the (loose overhand) knot. This will secure the knot.

This tie may be tied high or low. It drapes beautifully and has different variations for different looks even with a bias-shaped scarf.

Fan Bow

from a rectangular-shaped scarf

Place a rectangular-shaped scarf around your neck. Keep one end longer than the other.

Tie an overhand (half) knot in the scarf at the neck, having one end shorter.

Take the long end of the scarf and make a pleated fan. Do this by pleating the end back and forth, back and forth . . . until you get up to the overhand knot at the neck.

Tying Your Scarves

After getting the pleated fan up to the overhand half knot, take short end of scarf and bring it around the pleated fan.

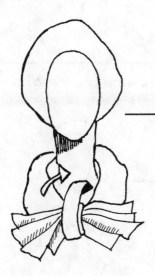

Continue to wrap the short end of the scarf around the pleated fan that you are holding in place.

Take the tail end (short end) and wrap it around until you have no more scarf. Tuck it in and under the loop that is formed to secure the fan bow.

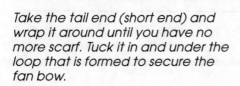

Half Bow

Put a rectangular-shaped scarf
around your neck with one end
longer than the other.

Double the longer end panel and
form a loop.

Holding the loop with one hand,
take the other end and bring it up
around the loop. Then tie a knot
around the loop.

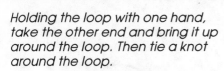

The Half Bow is then fluffed out
and arranged. It is also beautiful
with a bias-shaped scarf.

The Bow

Place a rectangular-shaped scarf around your neck.

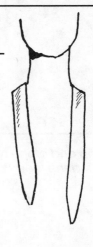

Having one end longer, tie a half knot.

Take the shorter end and fold it in half to make a loop.

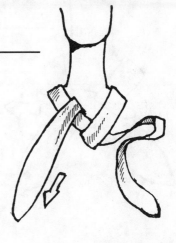

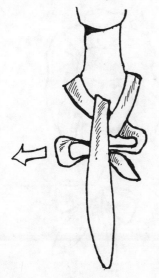

Hold the loop securely in one hand as you start to work with the long end.

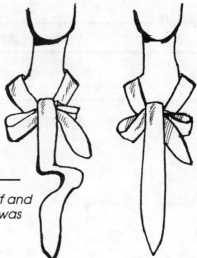

Take the long end of the scarf and wrap it around the loop that was formed.

Pull the long end of the scarf through the loop and form a bow.

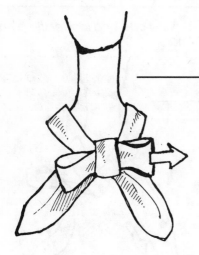

Batwings

Take a rectangular-shaped scarf
and fold it in half.

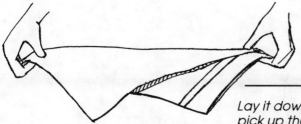

Lay it down on a flat table and
pick up the opposite ends
diagonally across from corner to
corner.

Put the folded straight edge of the
scarf against the neck, placing the
ends even in the front.

Tie a small square knot in the ends.

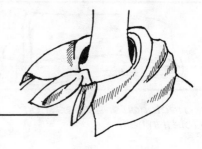

This tie can be placed on the side for a different look.

Turn the square knot to your back creating a cowl neckline collar.

Band-O-Tie

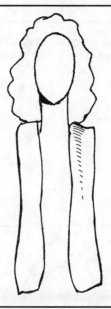

Drape a rectangular-shaped scarf around your neck.

Take a small rubber band between your first three fingers. Pinch and pull the two edges through the rubber band.

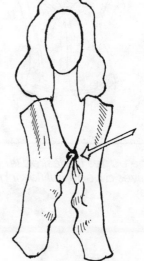

Secure the rubber band around the two edges. Then separate the edges and start to pull.

Pull the two edges out and up and this will form a bow that's very fluffy.

Variation of Band-O-Tie

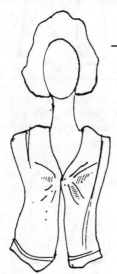

This same scarf tie can be done by reserving the rubber band to the back of the scarf. Take the rubber band under the two scarf panels. Pinch the edges together and pull the two through the rubber band.

Pull the edges to desired length. This gives a beautiful flowing ruffle dickey.

Snake

from one rectangular-shaped or one square-shaped folded into a bias-shaped scarf

If using a rectangular-shaped scarf, you may need to stand up to rotate it. The scarf will end up being twisted. If using a square-shaped scarf, fold to create a bias (about 2½ to 3 inches wide). Then twist to make a snake.

Many variations

Square knot tie from twisted square or rectangular-shaped scarf.

Twist tight around neck several times to make a Collar-Choker.

Double Collar is made the same way by using a longer rectangle.

Snake

from a two rectangular-shaped or two square-shaped folded into a bias-shaped scarf

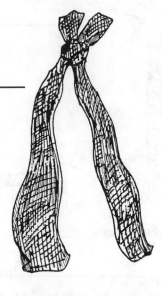

Tie two scarves together at one end to secure them for twisting.

If you don't have someone to hold the tied end, hook it over a nail or knob and then twist the ends of the scarves over each other. Twist over and over until you get to the end.

Use this snake around your head and, if it's long enough, use it around your waist.

Cross Link Tie

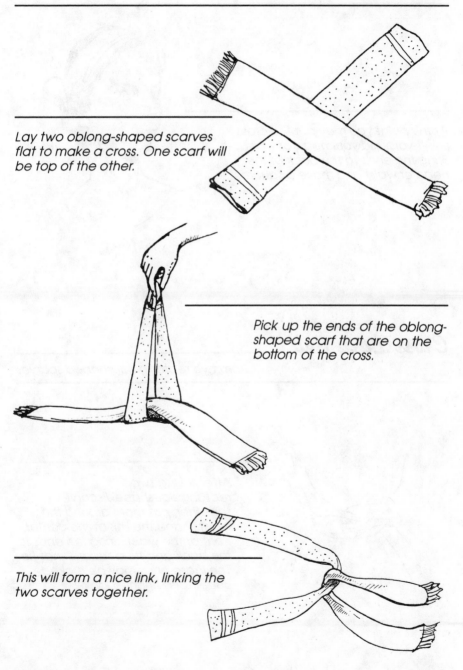

Lay two oblong-shaped scarves flat to make a cross. One scarf will be top of the other.

Pick up the ends of the oblong-shaped scarf that are on the bottom of the cross.

This will form a nice link, linking the two scarves together.

Cross Link Turban

from two rectangular-shaped scarves

At this point you may put the cross link tie around your head or waist. Bring the ends to the back of the head or waist and make a square bow.

Cross Link Belt

from two rectangular-shaped scarves

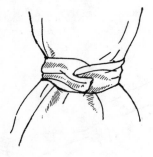

After linking two rectangular-shaped scarves together, put them around the waist. Place the link at the center front of the waist. Bring the ends to the back and tie a square knot tie. The loose ends may be tucked under for a finished look.

Cross Link Head Wrap

from one rectangular-shaped scarf

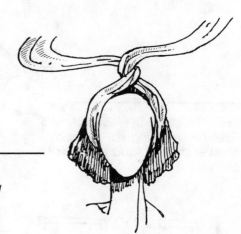

With center of oblong-shaped scarf at the back of head, bring the end up to the front of forehead. The ends are twisted around each other twice and pulled to make a link.

Take each end to the back of the head and tie a knot. The ends may be tucked in or hang loose.

Drape Neckline

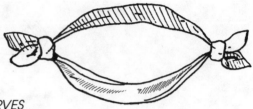

RECTANGULAR-SHAPED SCARVES
Take two rectangular-shaped
scarves and tie square knots on
both ends.

SQUARE-SHAPED SCARVES
Take two square-shaped scarves
and fold them with the right side
showing out.

Fold each scarf to about 2½ to 3
inches wide.

The final look of the Draped
Neckline is very feminine. You may
place the square knots on the
shoulders. Or you may want to put
one knot at the back of your neck
and the other one in the front,
giving a very deep neckline.

Florette _____

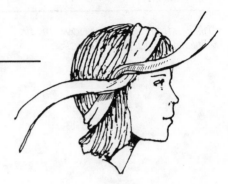

Put a rectangular-shaped scarf around your head, neck, or waist and tie an overhand knot.

Pull the knot as tight as you wish. You may even tie a square knot if you wish.

Take the ends and twist, forming a tight coiled snake. When finished twisting the snake, tie a small half-knot in the ends to secure.

This illustration shows how this tie will look around the neck.

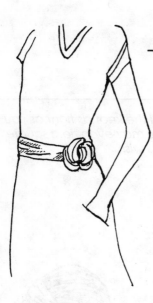

The twisted coil snake is wrapped around and around the knot, forming a florette. The florette may be finished by pulling the ends through the center of the circle from the back to wrap around and tuck the ends in. Or you may finish by not wrapping about a third of the ends so that when the ends are tucked through the center of the circle the tails are hanging from the back of the florette.

Tying Your Scarves

Plat Wrap

from a long rectangular-shaped scarf or sash

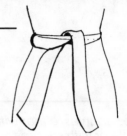

A long rectangular-shaped scarf works best for this belt (or else tie two rectangles together). Tie a half-knot after wrapping around the waist.

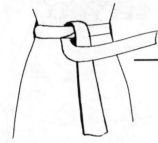

You will be using the two ends to do the braid, and the band around the waist will be the third strand. Take the bottom end and cross over the top panel.

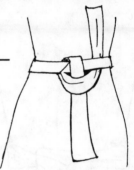

This strand is then brought up under the waistband panel. Then repeat by bringing that top strand down over the waistband panel.

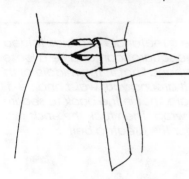

This braid is repeated again and again. Remember, you are only working with two panels and the words are: OVER, UNDER, UP then DOWN.

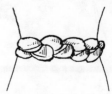

Waist and Body Wraps

Use three scarves, either with rectangle or with square folded on the bias. Secure them at one end by tying together and tie off the other end. Wrap around your waist or body or hat and tie ends.

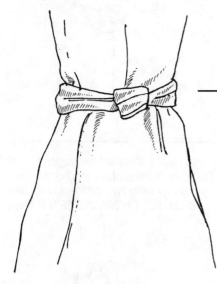

Take a rectangle or a bias-folded large square scarf and tie a loose overhand knot in the middle of it. Put it around your waist and tie a square knot in the back to secure the wrap. Then tuck the ends under the created belt.

Buckle Belt or Necklace _____

from a rectangular-shaped scarf

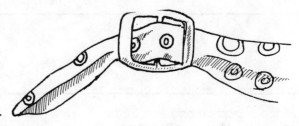

Take a rectangular-shaped scarf
and put it through a buckle.

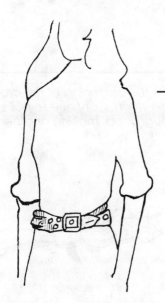

Feed one end of the scarf through
the buckle at a time, and place it
around the waist. It can be pulled
tight or worn loose and lower on
the hips.

This can make a beautiful, colorful,
and unusual necklace.

Crochet Chain Stitch Necklace or Waist Belt

from a rectangular-shaped scarf

Make a loop on one end of the scarf by pulling another loop up through to make a knot around the loop.

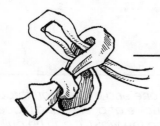

This is the beginning of the crochet chain stitch. Continue to pull scarf through loop, making another loop.

Continue chain to desired length, then pull the end through to tie off the chain.

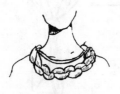

Necklace

Waist Belt

Single Bandeau

from a rectangular-shaped or square-shaped scarf

Fold a rectangular-shaped scarf around bust into a bandeau and knot in back. Or fold a square-shaped scarf into a rectangle, about 6 inches wide, and secure with a square knot in back.

Bandeau Tandem

from two rectangular-shaped scarves

Using two rectangular-shaped scarves, fold and wrap one around bust in bandeau style and knot in the back. Interlocking scarf over the bosom as tandem, loop it around the middle of bandeau front and tie as a halter around the nape of neck.

Bandeau Halter

from a rectangular-shaped or bias-shaped scarf

Take two rectangular-shaped scarves and tie them together, end to end, with a square knot. Position the square knot in the middle of the bust and start wrapping.

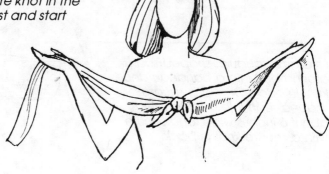

Wrap the ends around the bust to the back. The scarves are crossed behind the back. Then pull the ends to the front under the arms.

After going under the arms and bringing the ends up and around to the front, tie the ends with a square knot at the nape of the neck.

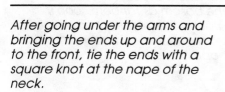

Square Knot

Start with a square-shaped scarf.

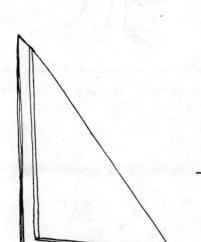

Fold to make a triangle. Begin by putting the triangle around the neck. (This is for the dominant right hand. Can be tied the same way starting with the left side.)

Take the right side-tail and cross it over the left side-tail.

Bring the right end over, then under and up through the left side-tail, and TIE.

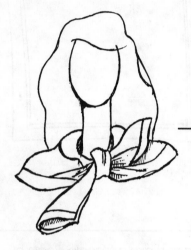

Then bring the LEFT end OVER (and under up through the right side-tail) and TIE.

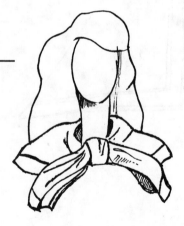

The square knot tie—completed from a square-shaped scarf with the tie in front.

Rotate the square knot to the back of the neck and you create a draping cowl collar that looks like a triangle. If starting with the right hand, remember: Right end over left and TIE, then left and over right and TIE.

Tying Your Scarves

Bandit

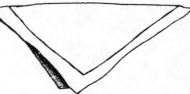

Fold to make a triangle from a square-shaped scarf.

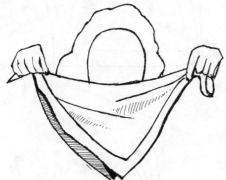

Bring the triangular-shaped scarf around the face, just below the eyes and over the nose and mouth. Take the ends to the back of the head and cross them. Then bring the ends to the front of the neck.

With the ends pulled to the front of the neck, tie a square knot under the chin. Take the ends up and around and tuck them in.

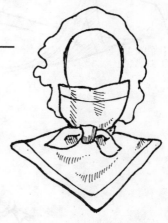

The top folded edge of the scarf across the nose is then pulled down over the knot. This covers the square knot and makes a wonderful turtleneck collar to fill in an open neckline.

Batwings

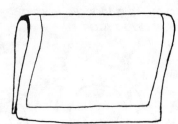

Place a square-shaped scarf on a
surface and fold it in half.

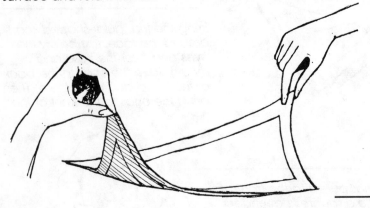

Pick up the opposite ends
diagonally across from each other.

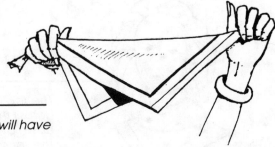

The square-shaped scarf will have
two triangle points.

Put the folded straight edge of the scarf against the neck, placing the ends even in the front.

Tie a square knot in the ends.

Batwing Headwrap

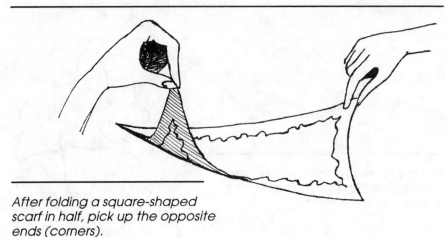

After folding a square-shaped scarf in half, pick up the opposite ends (corners).

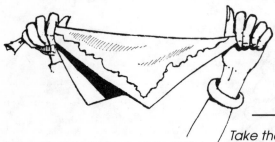

Take the straight edge that is folded and put it around the front of your head.

Pull the two ends (corner edges) to the back of the neck. Tie a square knot and arrange the points of the batwings.

Accordion

Lay the scarf flat and fold as an accordion with the width you wish. (From 2 to 4 inches.)

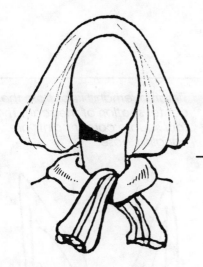

Put the scarf around the neck with the ends in the front. The accordion is in place to tie a half-knot.

Take each end one at a time and pull it up under the neckband from the bottom to the top.

Butterfly Tie

Lay a square-shaped scarf flat,
grab the center and pick up with
finger.

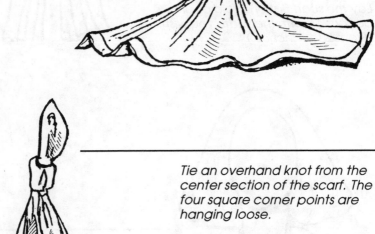

Tie an overhand knot from the
center section of the scarf. The
four square corner points are
hanging loose.

Take two ends of the square and
fold as a triangle, with the right
side of scarf on the outside and
the knot is on the underside.

Butterfly Dickey

from a square-shaped scarf

The ends of the Butterfly Tie are taken to the back of the neck and tied in a square knot. The knot may be placed at the back of the neck for a Dickey, or for another variation, to one side of the neck.

Butterfly Sarong

from a square-shaped scarf, jumbo size (45 inches × 45 inches or larger)

The Butterfly Tie can also be done with a jumbo square-shaped scarf (45 inches × 45 inches or larger) around the waist. Bring the ends to one side of the waist to tie a square knot. This makes a beautiful Sarong as it drapes across the hips.

Hal-blouse-ter _____

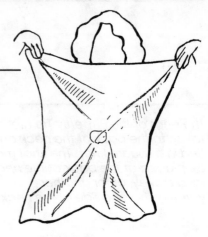

from a square-shaped scarf

Make a halter blouse from a jumbo
square by tying an overhand knot
in the center section of the scarf.
This is like the Butterfly tie. Then
pick up the ends from the two
straight edge corners.

Tie these corners around the back
of the neck.

Then take the other two straight
edges and tie around the waist.

Roll the bottom edges under for a
halter or tuck them into your skirt or
belt for a blouse effect with a suit
jacket.

Tying Your Scarves

Décolletage Halter

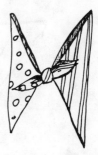

Make a triangle at each of two large square-shaped scarves. Lay the two triangles on a flat surface with the triangle points touching each other. Tie these together making four points. Tie a square knot.

The small square knot that was tied is placed between the breasts. The two top corners are brought up behind the nape of neck and tied with a square knot.

The remaining scarf corners are brought low to the back. Tie another square knot in these ends. Secure the loose edges by folding and tucking them under for a smooth look.

Secret Shawl Knot

from a square-shaped scarf, jumbo size (45 inches × 45 inches or larger)

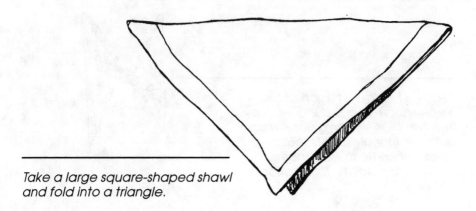

Take a large square-shaped shawl
and fold into a triangle.

Put the shawl around the
shoulders. Bring the ends of the
square under the arms.

The ends of the square-shaped scarf are tied into a square knot at the back.

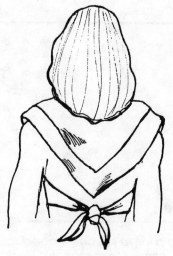

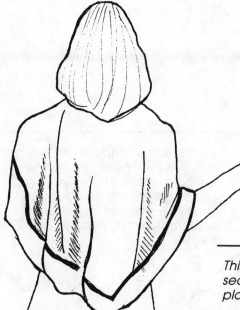

This Secret Shawl Knot tie is a secure way of always keeping it in place.

Armadillo Wrap

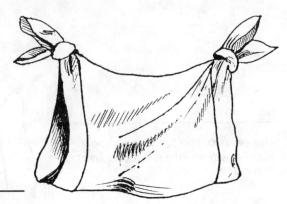

Using a large square-shaped scarf, fold to make a rectangle. Tie the two corners together on each end. If there is a right and wrong side to the scarf or shawl, be sure to fold so that the right sides face each other.

Take the scarf and turn it right side out. Then you have created two armhole openings. The knots on each end are under your arms. You have created an Armadillo wrap for warmth, comfort, and beauty.

Throw Wraps

from a square-shaped scarf, jumbo size
(45 inches × 45 inches or larger)

ONE-SHOULDER THROW
On Shoulder Throw Drapes, the
shawl or scarf may be placed over
or under your belt.

UNDERARM KNOT THROW
This is best if it's folded to about a
10-inch width before draping. The
square may be folded on the bias
and placed over the shoulder. If
not tied, the ends can be placed
under the belt at the opposite hip.

TWO-SHOULDER TRIANGLE THROW
The jumbo square is folded into a
triangle. The point of the triangle
can be placed to the center front
or the side front. Tie a square knot
in the back. Or, after crossing the
ends at the back, bring them to
the front.

Twist Waist Wrap

from a rectangular-shaped or large square-shaped scarf

When using a large square-shaped scarf, fold to get a bias shape. You'll want it between 6 and 8 inches wide.

Wrap around waist, and twisting as you wrap; tie a square knot at the end and tuck in ends. When using a rectangular-shaped scarf to do the same thing, just don't make a bias fold to start. Tie off ends and tuck.

When using a rectangular-shaped scarf, do the same loose twist as you are wrapping. As it is wrapped it's crossed. You can wear this around your hips (if your hips are small enough).

Tying Your Scarves

3. Using Clips to Enhance Your Scarves

A scarf clip is something that is very versatile and the scarf adaptor clip is even more useful. When one uses the scarf clip adaptor for either a brooch or an earring, you can turn your jewelry into a beautiful scarf clip. A scarf clip adaptor works wonders on fragile silk, because you do not have to pierce your silk scarf with a brooch. You can still wear your brooch, just attach it to the scarf clip adaptor and you don't have to pin into the fabric.

Many people who wear pierced earrings have told me that they have so many one-of-a-kind earrings left over from the pierced earring they have lost. By using the scarf clip earring adaptor, you can utilize that one earring that you have left and turn it into a scarf clip.

When using the scarf clip, you can add a personal signature to an outfit. The versatility of using the unique scarf clip adaptors will add so much to your style. When using a scarf clip you can think of using it, rather than a knot. In other words, you will use a scarf clip in place of tying a knot. When learning to use a scarf clip adaptor, or a conventional scarf clip, it is very important to understand exactly how to hold the clip.

Review the illustrations and the instructions on the following pages, and practice, practice, practice your creations. Most of all the scarf ties in the book can be created with your scarf clip adaptor. It is another variation of a conventional scarf tie. If you will remember that all you're doing is replacing the knot of a tie with the scarf clip adaptor. In doing this you will be able to create your own scarf clip magic. Have fun accessorizing with your new scarf magic clip adaptor.

Standard Scarf Clip _____

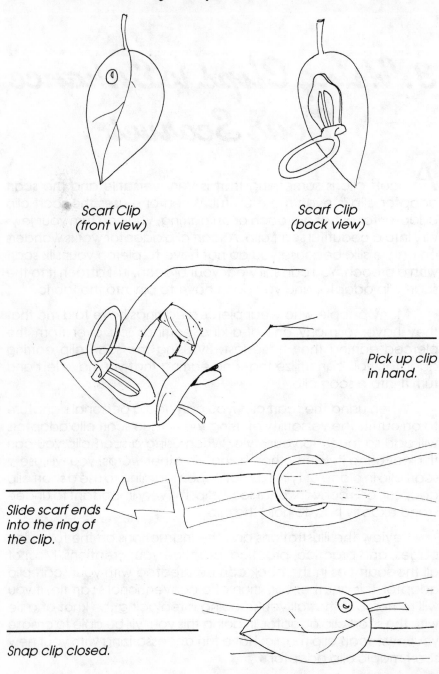

Scarf Clip
(front view)

Scarf Clip
(back view)

Pick up clip
in hand.

Slide scarf ends
into the ring of
the clip.

Snap clip closed.

Scarf Pin Adaptor

Scarf Pin Adaptor

Brooch

Insert stem of brooch into the
clutch on the clip adaptor.

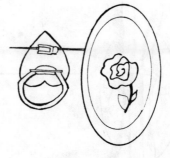

Side view of brooch and clip
adaptor

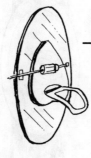

Back view of closed brooch with
clip adaptor. Fasten the stem of
the brooch to the brooch catch.

Place ends of scarf through the ring of the clip.

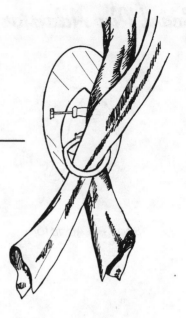

Slide adaptor up to desired area.

Snap adaptor closed.

Using Clips to Enhance Your Scarves

Scarf Clip Adaptor

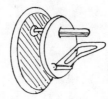

Place pierced earring post into the hole of the adaptor.

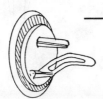

Push earring in until it touches the adaptor.

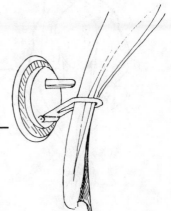

Place ends of scarf through the ring of the scarf. Slide up scarf to desired area.

Snap clip adaptor closed.

Cow-Girl-Clip

Fold a square-shaped scarf into a triangle, or use a rectangular-shaped scarf. Arrange the scarf around your neck so that the ends are equal.

Take the ends of the scarf down through the ring of the clip. Pull the clip up the scarf to the desired spot.

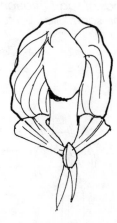

Arrange the scarf clip and snap it closed. When you have a lightweight (silk) scarf, to keep the clip from slipping, tie an overhand knot on one panel up under the clip.

Using Clips to Enhance Your Scarves

Clip-O-Bow

from a rectangular-shaped scarf

Drape a rectangular-shaped scarf around your neck.

Take the scarf clip or magic clip adaptor to the area you wish to pull the scarf through. Pinch the edges of the scarf together.

Place the clip to the scarf and pull edges through the ring. Take both edges of scarf that you have pinched together and separate them as you pull the scarf through the ring of the clip.

The clip will automatically move to the place you wish to stop it. When it's in place, clamp it closed and fluff.

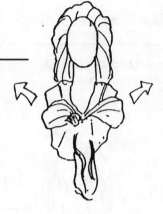

Arrange and fluff the bow as you wish . . . in the front or to the side of the neck.

Using Clips to Enhance Your Scarves

Cameo-Clip

Drape scarf around neck making sure to even up the ends in front. Put each end of the scarf through the ring of the clip.

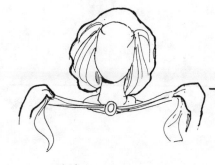

As you pull each end of the scarf in opposite direction, the scarf clip will slide up to the neck.

Bring each end of the scarf around to the back of the neck. One end of the scarf should be on each side. Either tie a square knot in the ends or tuck in the ends.

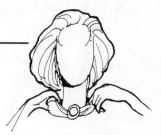

Snap the scarf clip closed. This makes a beautiful cameo choker.

Ascot-Clip

from a square or triangular-shaped scarf

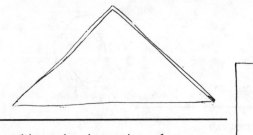

Use a triangular-shaped scarf or square-shaped scarf folded into a triangle.

Place scarf around neck.

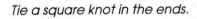

Tie a square knot in the ends.

Rotate the square knot to the
back of the neck and pick up the
folded edge in the middle of the
scarf. Take the scarf clip in your
free hand.

Pull the scarf down through the
ring of the clip.

Spread the part of the scarf that
was pulled through the clip. This
will make an ascot effect.

Snap the scarf clip closed to
secure.

Clip Half Bow

Shown with square-shaped scarf—can also be done with
rectangular-shaped scarf

When using a square-shaped scarf

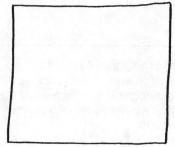

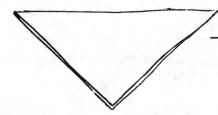

Fold into a triangle

Put it around your neck keeping
the ends even.

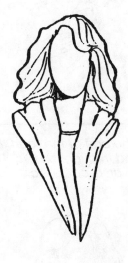

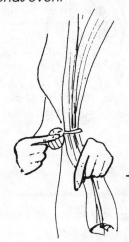

Push the ends of the scarf down
through the ring of the clip.

Using Clips to Enhance Your Scarves

Place the clip in the position you wish it to be.

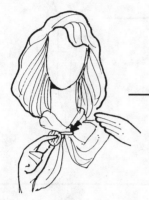

Take one end of the scarf and bring it up around and down into the ring. This forms a puff on one side.

Snap the clip closed and open up the puff of the half bow.

Clip Full Bow

from a square-shaped or rectangular-shaped scarf

Follow the preceding steps for the Clip Half Bow when doing the Clip Full Bow.

The second free hanging end is brought up, around, and down into the clip ring.

Station Clip Trick

from a rectangular-shaped scarf—trick for any shape scarf

Put a rectangular-shaped scarf
around your neck.

Select a safety pin with a stem
long enough to make a bar for the
scarf clip to slide under and pin it
inside your garment.

Take the scarf clip and slide it up
the panel of scarf opposite the
safety pin bar side. The scarf end
will go through the clip ring.

Slide the ring of the clip that has
the scarf through it under the stem
of the safety pin.

Using Clips to Enhance Your Scarves

The other end of the scarf that comes around your neck is then pulled through the half of the clip ring that's showing under the safety pin bar.

The clip is closed and the scarf is anchored. This clip trick with the safety pin is one that can be used with most of the clip ties. The beauty of the trick is that it will keep your scarf exactly where you want.

Or use a scarf clip

The two end corner edges are pulled together and put down through the ring of the scarf clip.

The clip should slide up to the side of one ear. It needs to be tight to the head. Secure clip and snap it closed.

Batwing Clip Headwrap

Follow steps for the Batwing (in chapter 2). However, rather than tying a square knot, use your scarf clip.

Cross Link Head Clip

Follow for the Cross Link Turban (in chapter 2). But rather than tying a knot at the side of the head, use the scarf clip. The Cross Link is at the top of your head. Bring the ends together and pull them up to the side of one ear. Pull all four ends of scarves down through the ring of the clip. Secure the scarf clip by sliding it up to one side of the ear. It should be arranged close to the head. Then snap the clip closed.

4. Caring For Your Scarves

A scarf can be a lifetime accessory with proper care and handling. Although different scarves are made of different materials, they all have common care requirements. Treat your scarves with tender loving care and you can have lifelong enjoyment of these statement-making accessories.

Scarves come in many different fabrics and blends. Some scarves are made of silk, ranging in weight from the very light to the considerably heavier. Others are made of cotton, cotton blends, or polyester. Heavier scarves are often made of different weights of wool and flowing challises. Yet even with all the different fabrics, blends, and weights you can find in scarves, there are certain basic principles of scarf-care and scarf-handling that apply to any kind of scarf.

Cleaning Your Scarves

You will find cleaning instructions on the labels of most scarves. These labels will tell you to "Dry Clean Only." However, I have had very good success hand-washing my silk and cotton scarves and even some of my wool ones.

If you decide to wash your silk and cotton scarves by hand, be sure to use a cold water wash with a mild soap such as Ivory Liquid or Woolite. Dip the scarf into the cold water, up and down, up and down, up and down. Never wring the scarf out while you're washing it.

Once you have washed the scarf in the cold water wash, rinse it thoroughly in clean, cold water at least twice. Place a clean, lint-free, white towel on a flat surface and blot the scarf until you get it as dry as possible.

Then hang the scarf up by its ends and let it dry over the bathtub. It should be hung on a plastic hanger with plastic clothes clips. Never hang a washed scarf on a metal or wooden hanger because of the risk of rust or splinters. After the scarf is thoroughly dry, steam-iron it at the recommended temperature for the fabric you are pressing.

Every wool scarf I have seen has a "Dry Clean Only" tag on it. I recommend, especially if the wool scarf is large, that it be dry cleaned professionally the first time. After the colors are set, a result of the first cleaning, then you should be able to do a handwash. I have hand-washed my wool scarves, but you MUST be very careful.

Wash your wool scarves the same way you wash your silks and cottons, with a mild soap and cold water. It is important to pat and roll dry your wool scarf in a large towel. Press dry with your iron set on low wool heat.

All synthetic scarves can be hand-washed, and the polyester ones are usually machine-washed. Do remember, the machine should be on the gentle cycle and you should always use cold water. Most man-made fibers seem to stain easily, so be sure to take care of the soiled areas immediately.

Never store a dirty scarf with a clean one. Keeping your scarves clean will make them last a lifetime.

Storing Your Scarves

I suppose you've probably done what I have when storing your scarves. Have you pressed your scarves . . . folded them neatly and then put them away in a drawer, just to be forgotten?

Having scarves stored in a drawer meant they were out of sight. Do you know the old adage, "Out of sight, out of mind?" It's true; if your scarves are not accessible you will not wear them as much as you should.

I have purchased every type of accessory gadget and hanger to store my scarves. I've tried them all, I must admit, but to no avail. But now, through the process of much time, thought, and effort, I've put together the Scarf Magic Hanger and the Scarf Magic Travel Roll.

These are ideas for storing your scarves at home and while traveling. The best thing about these tips is that they will not cost you a lot. You'll be able to put these projects together with little time. You should already have most of the items you'll need to make the Magic Hanger and Magic Travel Roll.

The Scarf Magic Hanger

Let me describe to you how you can take a full-size garment hanger and turn it into a **Scarf Magic Hanger.**

You'll need:
1. large plastic full hanger
2. Scotch tape
3. tissue paper
4. a piece of cloth (old sheet or muslin about 6 feet long by 28 inches wide
5. four clothes pins

Starting about 1 inch from the end of the hanger, wrap a strip of Scotch tape several times around the bottom bar. Leave the tape on the dispenser, and let the tape extend from the hanger about 3 inches. Cut the tape, leaving the 3 inches hanging down.

About 1 inch from the other end of the hanger, wrap Scotch tape in the same manner. Take the tape and wrap it around the bar several times, securing it just as you did on the other end of the hanger. Let the tape extend from the hanger about 3 inches and cut it off.

Wrap a third piece of Scotch tape around the middle of the garment hanger's bottom bar in the same manner as both ends. Be sure to let the tape hang 3 inches before cutting it from the dispenser.

The Scarf Magic Hanger

Plastic garment hanger with
Scotch tape extending out
approximately 3 inches.

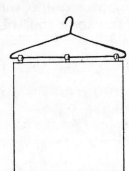

White tissue paper secured to
Scotch tape.

Wrap tissue paper around hanger
until it is approximately 1 inch in
diameter.

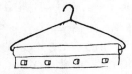

Four pieces of tape made into
double sided tape.

The end of the tissue paper should
end up on the bottom of the bar.

After you have wrapped the three separate strips of tape on the bottom bar of the garment hanger, take a piece of soft white tissue paper and cut it as wide as the bottom bar of the garment hanger (usually about 15 inches). Place one end of the tissue paper against the bar of the garment hanger. The three pieces of Scotch tape will stick to the tissue paper. Press the Scotch tape firmly onto the paper to hold it securely.

Start to wrap the tissue paper around the bottom bar of the garment hanger. Keep wrapping the tissue paper around and around until it is about 1 inch in diameter.

When you are making your last layers with the tissue paper, take four pieces of Scotch tape about 2 inches long and make out of each piece a **double-sided tape** by folding one end around to the other end. Equally space the four pieces of tape along the underside of the tissue paper and secure each piece tightly to the part of the tissue paper that has already been rolled up on the bar of the garment hanger. **Be sure that the end of the tissue paper ends on the bottom of the garment hanger bar and not on the top of the bar.**

This will make you a nice **Scarf Magic Hanger** over which you can hang your scarves. After you have pressed your scarves, just store them on the garment hanger. They will be free of wrinkles and folds—and ready to wear. To accomplish this, there is a special way of hanging your scarves on the **Scarf Magic Hanger.**

Arranging Your Pressed Scarves on the Scarf Magic Hanger

Now that you have made your **Scarf Magic Hanger,** let's talk about arranging your pressed scarves to be stored on it.

Use a soft, white, lint-free piece of cloth (an old white sheet or 2 yards of inexpensive muslin material usually works quite well). Cut the material into a rectangular shape about 6 feet long by 28 inches wide. If the muslin is 56 inches wide, cut it in half lengthwise and you'll have two pieces to be used on two different hangers. This will become your **Scarf Magic Cloth.**

Fold the **Scarf Magic Cloth** in half lengthwise and press it to make a visible crease in the middle. You may wish to iron this crease into the cloth. Lay the **Scarf Magic Cloth** on a bed and open it up full length.

Separate your scarves into two different categories: heavy nubby ones and smooth lightweight ones. In other words, put the heavier wools and challises together and the smooth, lightweight silks and cottons together.

Start with your **rectangular smooth and light scarves.** Place the longest smooth and light scarf adjacent to the center fold of the **Scarf Magic Cloth** and 1 inch from the top. This scarf should be fully extended. Place the second longest smooth and light scarf on top of the first one, about 3 inches down from the end of the first one. **Note: The edge of each scarf should be even with the center crease of the Scarf Magic Cloth.**

Continue this process of placing light and smooth rectangular scarves in descending lengths one on top of the other, with every scarf up against the edge of the center crease of the **Scarf Magic Cloth.** You can place up to 10 scarves on top of each other in this manner.

After you have placed all your rectangular smooth and light scarves on top of each other, fold your **square** light and smooth scarves in half and place them in the same manner on top of each other. You need to leave about 3 inches of each scarf exposed so that you can see all the scarves on your **Scarf Magic Cloth** at a glance. This in known as the **staggering technique.**

Take the part of the **Scarf Magic Cloth** that doesn't have any scarves on it and fold it over the staggered scarves you have arranged. Be sure to press the cloth against the scarves to hold them in place. This will keep them together when you pick up the hanger. Attach four evenly spaced plastic clothes pins to the **Scarf Magic Cloth** at the crease to hold everything in place.

Now you are ready to store your scarves. Place the **Scarf Magic Cloth** over the **Scarf Magic Hanger** you have made. You can then hang this magical accomplishment in your closet.

The beauty of the **Scarf Magic Cloth** is that your expensive and beautiful scarves will be protected from sharp wire coat hangers. The cloth will also act as a cover, keeping the scarves clean while they are hanging in your closet.

Arranging Your Pressed Scarves on the Scarf Magic Cloth

Soft, white cloth about 6 feet long by 28 inches wide, with its center crease, open and fully extended.

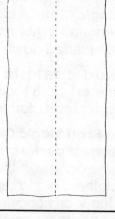

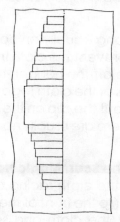

Sides are layed on top of each other. Right edges line up on the center crease of the cloth. Three inches of the top end of each scarf showing. This is the staggering technique.

Fold the side of the scarf cloth that does not have any scarves on it over your scarves. Attach four plastic clothespins on the cloth at the crease.

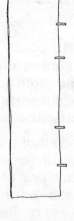

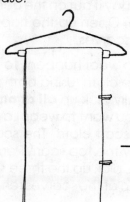

Place the scarf cloth over your Scarf Magic Hanger and hang it in your closet.

Use the same process as the one described above to make another **Scarf Magic Cloth** for your **heavier and nubbier scarves.** The only difference with the cloth for the heavier and nubbier scarves is that you may need to use something larger and heavier than a plastic clothespin to secure the scarves to the **Scarf Magic Cloth.** A plastic clothespin may not open wide or be strong enough to hold and keep the thicker textures and heavier materials pinned down.

If you decide to store both the lightweight scarf cloth and the heavier scarf cloth together on the same hanger, be sure to put the heavier scarf cloth on the bottom.

The **Scarf Magic Cloth** needs to hang equally on both sides of the hanger bar for balance. This will prevent the cloth from sliding off the hanger. If the cloth does slip off the hanger, take another clothespin and clip the two halves of the cloth together just below the scarf hanger bar. It is best to put the clip on the outside edge opposite the center fold, since there are usually no scarves in this area.

It is very **important** that you hang the **Scarf Magic Hanger** in the closet with the opening edges of the cloth facing out. The reason you want the cloth opening out (to the front of the closet) is that you can pick up either flap of the cloth and see your scarves at a glance. That way you can easily pick which scarf you want to wear.

Using Your Scarf Magic Cloth and Hanger

When you are ready to wear one of your scarves, remove the **Scarf Magic Cloth** from your closet and lay it out on the bed. Take the four clothespins off the scarf cloth. Open up the flap of the cloth—you will be able to see all your scarves.

Let's say that the scarf you want to wear happens to be the seventh one in your stack of ten on the cloth. Using both hands, one on each end of the group, carefully pick up **all at once** the top three scarves and leave the one you want to wear. Lay these three scarves on the free side of the scarf cloth. The scarf you want to wear (the seventh one) is now the top scarf. Remove it and pull it aside. Then, with both hands, pick up the three scarves you put aside and put them back on top of the scarves remaining on the scarf cloth. **Be sure to leave the 3-inch spacing between each scarf.** This will maintain the staggering technique that allows you to see all your scarves at the same time.

Cover up the staggered scarves with the free flap of the **Scarf Magic Cloth.** Re-attach the four clothespins and return the **Scarf Magic Cloth** to the **Scarf Magic Hanger.**

This **Scarf Magic Hanger** is very economical to make. You press your scarves once and then hang them. You don't have to dig through a drawer only to find that the scarf you want to wear is folded and wrinkled. You only need to press your scarves once when using this technique. Just press and hang on your **Scarf Magic Hanger.**

Using Your Scarf Magic Cloth and Hanger

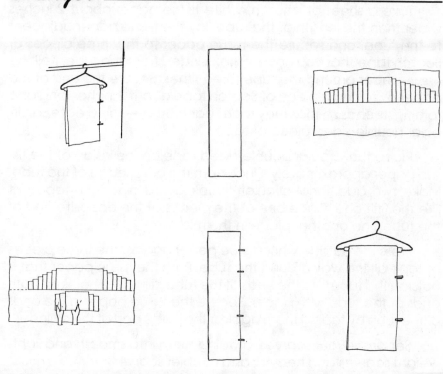

The Scarf Magic Travel Roll
How to Store Your Scarves When You are Traveling

I'd like to describe to you a technique for storing scarves when you are on the road. This is a technique that I have used quite successfully for a long time when traveling the world giving **Scarf-Tying Magic** Classes.

To make your **Scarf Magic Travel Roll** you'll need:

1. empty gift-wrap paper tube (about a 1-inch cylinder)
2. Scotch tape
3. white tissue paper

Begin with a gift-wrap paper **tube** approximately 1 inch in diameter and 18 inches long. Take a piece of Scotch tape and, starting about 1 inch from the end of the tube, wrap the tape around the tube. Then pull the tape out about 3 inches and cut it. Do the same in the middle of the tube and at the other end.

Take a sheet of smooth, white tissue paper about 2 inches wider than the length of the tube, lay the tissue paper adjacent to the tube, and secure the tissue paper to the three pieces of Scotch tape that you have left extended from the tube. Roll the tissue paper around the tube three times. Secure the end of the paper by taking a piece of Scotch tape about 2 inches long and folding its ends so that they meet each other—this creates a circular double-sided piece of tape.

Place the circular double-sided tape on the inside of the tissue paper approximately 1 inch from the outer edge of the tube. Make two additional circular double-sided pieces of tape just like the first one. Place one of the pieces at the opposite end of the tube and another piece in the middle.

Press the outside white tissue paper against the three pieces of tape all the way around the tube. Push the tissue paper that is outside the tube into the ends of the tube, filling the holes on both ends of the tube with paper. Secure the tissue paper in the ends of the tube by taping them against the inside part of the cylinder.

Separate your scarves, dividing them into smooth and lightweight scarves and heavier and nubbier scarves.

The Scarf Magic Travel Roll

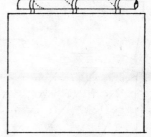

Use a gift-wrap paper tube 1 inch in diameter and 18 inches long.

Wrap tape around the tube, leaving about 3 inches extending.

Place white tissue paper about 2 inches wider than your tube onto the tape.

Roll the tissue paper around the tube about three times. Place three pieces of double-sided tape on the inside of the tissue.

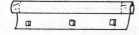

Press the loose ends of the tissue paper against the tube.

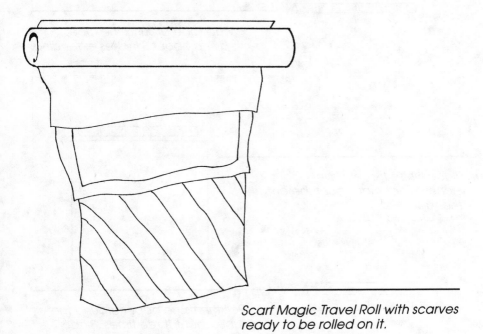

Push the tissue paper that is
outside the tube into the ends of
the cylinder and tape.

Scarf Magic Travel Roll with scarves
ready to be rolled on it.

Scarf Magic Travel Roll with scarves
rolled on it.

Caring for Your Scarves

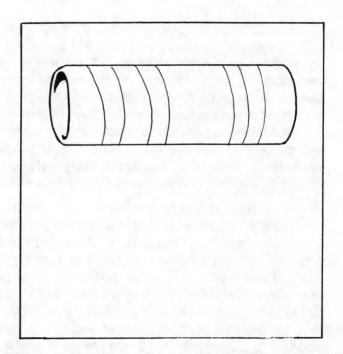

White cloth 20 inches by 20 inches.

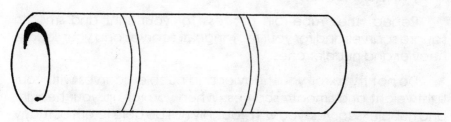

Wrap cloth around the scarves
and secure with two rubber bands.

Taking your longest smooth and lightweight rectangular scarf, place it fully extended on a flat surface. Put the next longest smooth and lightweight rectangular scarf on top of the first one about 3 inches down from the end of the first scarf. Repeat the process of placing smaller and smaller smooth and lightweight scarves on top of each other. Make sure that you leave about 3 inches of the underneath scarf showing so that you can see all of them at the same time. This is the same **staggering technique** used with the **Scarf Magic Hanger.** You can hold about 10 scarves on one **Scarf Magic Travel Roll.**

Now take the scarf roll tube that you have covered with white tissue paper and place it at the end of the first scarf. Be sure to center the tube in the middle of the first scarf. Start rolling the tube slowly from the one end of the first scarf to the beginning of the last scarf. When you have rolled to the beginning of the last scarf and have wrapped this last scarf around the cylinder once or twice to secure it onto the roll, you can pick up the rolled tube and let the rest of the scarves hand down. Finish rolling up the scarves to complete your **Scarf Magic Travel Roll.**

Cut a soft, white, lint-free cloth about 20 by 20 inches (muslin works fine). Wrap this cloth around the **Scarf Magic Travel Roll** to protect your scarves. Place two large rubber bands around the cloth to hold the scarves together on the roll. If you have a slender plastic bag you may want to store your **Scarf Magic Travel Roll** in it, but never store your scarves in a plastic bag for a long time. The plastic should have some holes in it so your scarves can breath. I have even stored my **Scarf Magic Travel Roll** in a pair of stockings in my suitcase for trips.

Repeat the "tube-roll" process for your light and smooth square scarves and for your rectangular scarves and your square heavier and nubbier ones.

Do not try to roll your heavier and nubbier scarves with your lightweight and smooth scarves. When you roll up your heavier and nubbier scarves, you will probably not be able to put as many together on one tube.

After you have all your different scarves rolled up on their tubes, they can be tucked into your suitcase or overnight bag. Make sure that nothing heavy is stored on top of the tubes. If the cylinder is crushed, it will cause the scarves to wrinkle and fold.

Conclusion

A scarf can add so much to your individual look. You can revitalize an old garment just by adding a simple new scarf and tying it in an unusual way. **Presto**—you have updated an outfit that is different, exciting, and reflective of your personal style. It can help you get interested all over again in that old wardrobe in your closet—or it can inspire you to go out and add new looks.

The scarf can accomplish so many things! It can give you new textures to add to your wardrobe. It can help you to vary the effect of your personal color pattern. It can create excitingly different and dynamically new optical illusions. It can help you to come across as formal or more informal, professional or romantic, mature or younger. It can highlight a feature or help you to conceal one. It can help you to enhance your basic body proportion or it can work to juxtapose colors for a dynamic new look. It can put you in the best light!

You can tie a scarf in one way and create one look—and then you can tie it in still another way to create another look. It's so simple! It's so versatile! Do you want to create the illusion of elegance? Do you want to create the illusion of simplicity? The only limit to what you can do with a scarf is your imagination!

So be courageous! Let your imagination go! Build a scarf wardrobe that enables you to be creative, different, and exciting. Get wrapped up in scarves and create a little magic!

Appendix: How To Make a Bias Scarf

If you would like to take a rectangular piece of fabric or even a rectangle scarf and turn it into a bias scarf, this is a very easy way.

As I said in the introduction of the book, I discovered this trick by accident when I didn't have enough material to make a scarf once. Take any size rectangular piece of fabric and turn it into a bias scarf.

The example illustrated used an old rectangle scarf. I didn't have any use for it as it was so I turned it into a bias scarf. I use these scarves now as ties around my neck and head.

Lay your fabric or scarf flat, with the right side of the material facing up. In other words, the wrong side (back side) of the fabric is toward the flat surface of the table.

You will be working with the fabric so that the inside will be the right side.

How to Make a Bias Scarf

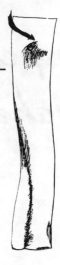

For a rectangle scarf 44 inches long by 5 inches wide, fold the 5-inch end piece over to the 44-inch long right outside edge.

As you bring the end piece to the outside edge, you fold it over, forming a triangle. Start stitching the two edges together at the corner. You are stitching the ending piece (width) of fabric to the outside (length) of fabric.

Now, as the two pieces of fabric are brought together, they are stitched.

How to Make a Bias Scarf

Continue bringing the outside length of fabric to the other (length) side and sew together.

The outside edges are sewn together. . .

You continue stitching. . .

Pulling the two outside panels together . . . still stitching the same way. . .

Still keeping on with your stitching, the outside pieces are sewn together.

Nearing the end, without interruption of your stitches, keep going.

At the end, leave an opening (whole left not sewn). Then you'll turn the fabric inside out so the right side of fabric is on the outside showing.

How to Make a Bias Scarf

Index of Ties

Turn your beautiful brooch or pierced earring into a unique scarf clip.

The Scarf Magic Clip Adaptor allows you to use your pins and earrings without putting a hole in your silk scarves or blouses.

☐ **YES!** I want to enhance my scarves with clips as described in Chapter 3 of *Scarf Tying Magic.* Please send me:

QTY	ITEM	GOLD (G) OR SILVER (S)	PRICE	TOTAL
	Scarf Magic Brooch Clip Adaptor		$14.95	
	Scarf Magic Pierced Earring Clip Adaptor		$14.95	
	Set of Scarf Magic Adaptors (includes 1 Brooch adaptor and 1 Clip adaptor)		$24.95	
	Scarf Tying Magic Video (indicate VHS or BETA)		$24.95	
	Please add $3.00 for shipping & handling.			$3.00
			TOTAL	

☐ Enclosed is my check for $ _____ .
☐ Please charge to my   ☐ VISA   ☐ MC   Exp. ___/___

Card No. _____   Signature _____

Please send my adaptors/purchases to:

NAME

ADDRESS

ZIP

PHONE (   )   DATE ___/___/___

Mail order and payments to: *

Bobbie Thompson
c/o Acropolis Books, Ltd.
2400 17th Street, NW
Washington, DC 20009

*Make checks payable to Image Reflections. Allow 3–6 weeks for delivery.